CW00750684

# Wan-Hu's Flying Chair

RICHARD MARGGRAF TURLEY was born in the Forest of Dean in 1970 and moved to Wales when he was seven. He teaches in the Department of English and Creative Writing, Aberystwyth University.

Also by Richard Marggraf Turley

*The Fossil-Box* (Cinnamon, 2007)
*Whiteout,* with Damian Walford Davies (Parthian, 2006)

# Wan-Hu's Flying Chair

RICHARD MARGGRAF TURLEY

CAMBRIDGE

PUBLISHED BY SALT PUBLISHING
14a High Street, Fulbourn, Cambridge CB21 5DH United Kingdom

© Richard Marggraf Turley 2009

The right of Richard Marggraf Turley to be identified as the
author of this work has been asserted by him in accordance
with Section 77 of the Copyright, Designs and Patents Act 1988.

Salt Publishing 2009
Reprinted 2010

Printed in Great Britain by the MPG Books Group, Bodmin and King's Lynn

Typeset in Swift 9.5 / 13

ISBN 978 1 84471 443 8 hardback

1 3 5 7 9 8 6 4 2

# Contents

# Acknowledgements

'Elisions' won the *Keats-Shelley Prize* for poetry in 2007. 'Afterlives' first appeared in *Agenda*, 'Billiard Ball' and 'Overheard' in *Planet*, 'A History of Explosions', 'Amulet', 'Umbels' and 'A Guide to the Stars' in *Poetry Wales*, and 'Thitherwards' and 'Toads' in *The Wolf*. 'Delft Tile' was first published in *Whiteout*, with Damian Walford Davies (Parthian, 2006). 'Steerage' is a joint composition with Kelly Grovier and first appeared in *New Welsh Review*. 'Slip' was commissioned for a radio programme broadcast in 2008 on Resonance FM.

# Landing Party

Saturday the second
we sailed from Salem,
laden with articles,

spankers brailed, the sea
a sweat of horned pout,
flying fish finning

like swallows. We laid into
the squall, seabirds
wheeling above the freak,

changing the sound of the sea.
A bucket of light loses
its brightness hoist on deck.

On the twenty-third,
we hauled our cargo ashore
with well-planed oars,

plantains and pumpkins,
up to our necks in the parallel
cries of tropick birds.

Around the ship, women
diving for sea-eggs, laid
out on the slimy black sand

with tripe and trumpet-
weed. A boar's head proved
the existence of pigs.

The women wore bracelets
and blue beads: roughly
with red faces, we begged

with others. In the shrubs
and creeping grass, they cut
our buttons for cocoa-nuts

and ears of corn, the air
beyond thermometers,
broken coral reaching

to fathoms. In the morning
we saw fewer birds,
our shot spent short of us.

The usual winds and weather,
skaerls and skarls,
flying fish like swallows.

# The Jade Corridor

You draw me to the planes
of a pendant older than pyr-
amids. I think its furious

stillness would rest on
your neck like silk. I imagine
you drinking from a jade

cup, sipping the wine's
pulse, hems weighed by plaques
of open-work and pierced

buckles. A burnished disc
brings the relief of flat
surfaces, its rice-pattern

opening the way to realms,
where to think is to occupy
space. The daggers lack

cruelty, edges too soft
to part flesh. Further along,
a high cabinet, a phoenix

and pyre carved in atoms.
Even you draw breath
at the conundrum of curves,

the feint of cursives scratched
in bone. A final glass brings
fluted forms, a polished

wheel of words, a lidless
vessel, a suit of stone
to keep the dead at bay. Locked

in, we leave past a gold
head-dress, a hat with winged
creatures quivering on springs.

# Suiting Up

These are the flooded salt-
marshes, navigated by terns,
and this, the hangar where

we store the suits. We've come
a long way since the lace-
ups of Mercury. You're looking

at the hard torso, bellow-
jointed with a zipper. The helmet's
the last shout, drinking straw

ready for the pull of lips.
At first we thought hooks
for hands, until we overcame

the problem of fingers
with kevlar, rubberized tips
for the impression of feeling.

You've found an optional
wrist mirror. And those
are nozzles for the nit-

rogen sighs. I urge you all,
consider the weight of bodies,
the delicious pitch and yaw,

water scaling off the pores.
Any suit worth its salt
should tighten like a corset.

You're alarmed; since the bladder
layer isn't pressured,
it won't 'pop' like balloons,

even if torn. That's quite it,
line up the parts—neck
to collar, shell to hinge, pin

to flange. The future's scrim
and chiffon, spandex stays
that push the breasts high,

impossibly. And the veil that hides
nothing, spaced inwardly—not
far off—the undarkening sky.

# Spindrift

They hint at things, these
hen tracks, scratched over
the waves' clenched

fingers. On the wharf,
a woman faces the sea's whisps;
she sees me, she doesn't

let on, or raise the gist
of smoke towards the bay:
inland, I hang words

in the filigrees of an apple
tree, a sugared bird churring
and I ask is it one slow

song, or many? Keying in
to its steady *oooo*, I catch surf,
the drogue's tow, a vessel

broaching to, far out. She's there,
drawing the moon's curtains;
unmoved, tidying the dark.

# Moon Songs

## 1. WAN-HU'S FLYING CHAIR

High above the mulberry
lake, washed with ink,
after the waving peach

blossom and the blast, above
the storked stars, what if
you'd cratered, broken

the well of gravity—
what if you'd arrived?
Wan-Hu, over the winter

birds, what would you
have made of the mag-
nificent desolation, the dry

mass? And, peering down
on the earth's bone
china-blue, marooned

in the deepest deep, what
strange songs clanged ears
before the torture of air?

## 2. ELIXIR

She observes the willow-
pattern world from her
cold kingdom, her jade

land. Gods, falling
as rocks in the ears.
Do not trust them,

Chang'e. Orioles sing
and elmkeys float through
the chrysanthemums;

saffron steams above
the firepot. Wrinkles
in the cherry lake

fooled you into flying,
left Hou Yi cut below
the bow-bent moon.

## 3. Seventh Moon

Suspended in the black
egg, Niu Lang longs
for his girl across

the celestial river. There,
she weaves clouds; and
he dreams of limbs

breaking the silk of
stars. Zhi Nu, meet her
on the magpie bridge,

feel again the elastic
collision of lovers,
the sky red over China.

# Elisions

*The firm of Boulton and Watt sent 132 engines
to the Caribbean between 1803 and 1830.*

Since you ask how
it begins, it begins
with elasticity

of steam, with sun
and planet gearing,
wax and resinous

bodies. It continues
with inequality
of pressure, with want

of wind and water.
It's put to work by the fly-
ball governors, Gale

and Long, and the am-
iable Pennant. I am
a man of sector and rack,

quadrant glass; I
calculate the economy
of heat. No, not

of planter class
myself. Look, these
latest drawings regulate

the speed of an engine,
describe the action
of vapour. Here, the descent

in the cylinder, and,
figure c, the condensate
and vacuum—and here,

here we find the endless
reservoirs. Each night,
this dream of dark

bodies. My valves move
by gears very similar
to Smeaton's.

# Forensics

What deceived us at first
was the distance between
them. The other con-

undrum, time, we cracked
by calling to mind flesh
maggots and the screw-

worm. That gave us five
days. You ask me, it was
she pitched the hike—

drawn, I imagine, *by the celeb-
rated light over the stairs
and spires.* Later, there must

have been cedar sparks
from the firepit, exploding
pockets of sap. Just picture

it. One minute, going
hammer and tongs; the next,
inundation, limbs every-

where, swollen sands rush-
ing through that dry bed
like nobody's business. How

do you drown in the desert?
After draining, the heat cured
them. Then insects, arriving

with their eggs. It takes
months, otherwise, for green
bones to push through.

Found them out on the plains,
some way north of the canyon's
throat. Hundreds of feet apart.

# Billiard Ball

Consider the round-
ness of the proposition:

think into the chafe
of planes, the bag-

atelle of balls, of angles
and the bounce of promis-

cuous cushions, each
collision a memory-

less kiss, love
spinning into balk space.

# Court Ladies of the Former Shu

Not as spiky as your domestic
scenes, Yin, the pavilions in dense
bamboo, or your celebrated bird-

on-a-bough; but these women will
be reckoned with. What feints
are conducted under their flower

hats, intrigues draped in thrown
silk? Not one of them looks you
in the eye. Old hierarchies, even

here in the heavenly quartet—
one bows, elbow raised to pour
wine—another, head barely

inclined, offers a still life of tray-
with-bottle. Peeled lychees
and jellies. You have to ask,

what is she thinking? It's the high-
handed beauties, purse-lipped,
that arrest us. Is that water-

weed on their lapels? They laugh,
as if gossiping about your coming
home, red-faced, broken, to Suzhou.

# Winter Wheat

*'According to the customs of Yizu, if war should occur
among villages, any woman can mediate by standing
between the fighting parties, agitating her skirts.'*
—*Customs of China*

On the banks of the Jinsha,
an open bundle of winter

wheat. In the high field,
women have abandoned

their chivving, scythes and long-
handed sickles shouldered,

wheeled wicker baskets
idle. They crane to watch

the spears and sticks
clatter and jab at her hems.

She sings, shaking the qun-
cloth with both hands

between the warring men
from her husband's village

and her own. She is awake
to the far-off birds, the orange

of the wutong tree. If they insist
on poking and parrying,

she will let slip her toused
gown, surrender her bare self.

# Life Classes

All I saw in the old masters
was bones—ramus,
sacrum, pelvis, the body's worse-

than-nakedness: warlike
radii poised over
cervical vertebrae, heroic

skulls pressed on spinal
columns, modest phalanges
cupped to form a perfect

*Venus pudica*. Now it's clear
how the drapery falls. Today,
a leaning male—such proud

nostrils. I'll bring him out
in charcoal. How can I be content
with fruit and bottles after this?

## 2. FEMALE NUDE WITH A MASK
*In the studio of Thomas Eakins, 1883*

Without smock and stays,
it's just the blind-
fold of the veil. Stranded,

her knuckles knit
in front of ilium and ischium,
her torso a man-

ipulation of light. He instructs
her not to move, an artist's
pupil before the catechizing

eye. Behind, the scaffold
of a chamber, a three-
legged stool.

# Afterlives

## 1. BLINK

*'Languille!'*[*]

The guillotined eyes
open like an oiled
machine, then sag
and seal.

*'Languille!'*

The dead hood
remembers. Just
eyes. See.

*'Languille!'*

Glaze.

[*] Convicted murderer, executed 1905

## 2. QUEEN OF SCOTS*

'Dogs will lick her blood' —JOHN KNOX

*Never undressed*
*before such company.*

We fixed a cloth to her
caule. It was the white neck
she wished to screen.
After the blood her skirts
trembled, the crowd
pushed and groaned.
We pulled off her garters:
there was Geddon for love
under her petticoats.

---

* Mary took her Skye terrier with her to execution, 1587

## 3. News from the Dead*

Good friends—
jigging up dead
weight and jerking
down hard with love
to speed the rope,
thumping the
breast till breath-
less in hope of still-
ing that awkward
pulse.
    I came to
under the dissector's
knife. Then poultices,
clysters, rub.

* Anne Greene, accused of infanticide, was executed in 1650. She was resus-
citated by the surgeon who collected her 'corpse' for medical purposes.
The title is that of the 1651 pamphlet relating the 'miracle'.

[22]

## 4. THE APPARENTLY DEAD*

After the fall
on Pudding Lane,
the prime conductor
with his marvel-
lous animal machine—
jar and poles jumping
the gap-
      spark. De-
fibbing—
o the shock of life.

---

* In 1774, a three-year-old girl fell from an upper-story window onto
flagstones. After she was pronounced dead an apothecary resuscitated
her with a portable electrostatic generator.

# A History of Explosions

1. TAIL OF THE DEVIL

*'Something extraordinary happened here.'* —A. R. HILDEBRAND

Clasts of rock, rivers
of glass, a neck-
lace of springs at Chicx-

ulub. Then—
the wrap of dust
and the furious ex-

tinction, shocked
quartz calculated
in tens to the powers of.

## 2. WAN-HU

*'Perhaps the first astronaut.'* —NASA

Look, the bam-
boo wings of Wan-
Hu's flying chair.

The air is still
beneath the sky's
cloudy river,

and strange birds
peer out
from the jujube

thorns. The sudden
rush of torches,
the almighty

bang. Silence, space.

## 3. KUZKA'S MOTHER

*'A remote, indistinct and heavy blow, as if
the earth had been killed.'* — Soviet cameraman

All the earth's fires
in one place,
fins and nacelles

like Ming's rocketship,
the illusion of fast
atoms. Then

the world un-
folds, its flash in the pan
a percentile of sun.

## 4. RX J0822-4300 (Neutron Star)

*'Astronomers are at a loss for words.'*

Other flaming bodies
careen to slower
destinations.

This one's a cosmic
cannonball—all
those years

of burn, then
nothing to hold
on to.

# Castles

## 1. ST BRIAVELS

Pron. *Brĕv-ĭls,* rhymes with 'devils'

In the forest's subtle
centre, new throats
of growth — longwaves

of character — rootle
the visible horizon.
Back in the forest's bone

beds, under the ghastly
postures of trees, I
perch above the curious

stones of Wilton Bridge,
joggled between cut-
waters and crossroad

divines. Hassock and alder
and chalybeate springs
bring the injured

windows of St Briavels.
Giddy under demi-
rounders, I girdle walls

and dry towers, lean to
the fortified apple
of Hudknoll's Wood.

There's such ringwork
in these stones, unlevied
from pontage and pick-

age. The must in the press
blurs the chimney's
counterforts and carved

corbels, my cantilevered
thoughts calling time
beneath the scriptured beam.

## 2. GOODRICH

After the long slide
through the forest's junc-
tions and green light,

the ground gives way
to relics of epochs,
correl and hinged shell.

Parked up, I kneel
to jacks in the shale
linking Blorenge

and Dean beneath
the arches of Good-
rich. Shocked by the scale

of the ground's dis-
locations, I roost on
the prominence, cooled

by fishbone leaves, hail
the lava top of Titter-
stone Clee, teeter

on the roasting strata,
survey the butt-
ressed walls; and pause

at the blood of the lady's
ashlared tower, split-
ting angles *ad absurdum*.

# Three Palettes

### 1. IN THE CAMPO DI SAN POLO

I meant sooner to have congratulated
you on the *Supper*; the supreme harmony

of proportions, the impression of infinite
space. No-one does suppers quite like

you. Me? An embarrassment of choice.
That one, perhaps; or that? Right play

of light, she'd stretch to a Giulia, a *donna
di salda virtù*, if ever there was one. I have

an idea for a scene. There will be war.
Horses, gods, giants. In the background,

several heads, a duke's coronet, a skull
cap; a serpent creeping to the legs of

my Lady. You know her—last year's bawd
in a highbacked chair, a string of pearls

to set her off, the slope of her shoulders
brilliantly done. I'm known for anatomy

(Jacopo's *Venus* hangs like a sack). I'm told
you're lost in contemplation of the *Judgement*;

remember, in fat times anyone can be
good. Now, there's a girl; toss her

a few *scudi*, stick her in front of an arras—
Io fleeing, Zeus turned to a cloud.

## 2. UNTITLED

I believe you are in his study, letting him con-
template the trick of you. If I know him,

he will rise to the challenge of your puz-
zle. Now your clothes fall to the rug's

palette, beneath the silver standard lamp.
I can feel his *mirar fiso*, picture the sound

you make, the lines you describe. You
never look at him from the place he

sees you. Soon there will be art. Please,
notice the modest oil-on-board, wide-eyed

above the bookcase, varnished with pine
resin, next to the horseman glimpsed

through the garden gate; the ring-
lets and golden ties, fat over lean — his first

nude, done wet-on-wet with stoat-hair,
her pious dark garments draped over a chair,

beneath the silver standard lamp. Tastes
change; my dear, he'll do you differently.

### 3. Old Master

At first, I painted whatever fell to hand:
kitchen tools, skulls, a brace of pheasants—

find some space between the easels
and incunabula, the relics of days; what

do you say to the ashes of a martyr,
a twig from the burning bush?—before

moving on to livelier sittings. Burghers
and their wives, together or singly. Not

sure favourite's quite the word; but that's her
leaning there, almost dry. Before we began,

I fed her grapes. She stood for it on a tiny
moon, a dusty promontory in the gardens,

her eyes an escalation of love. Much like others,
preserved in folding doors; except, instead

of the customary drop of hills and trees,
I plumped for the dark, the principal light

formed from gold braids pulling on her hair.
If these bones and teeth could talk. My latest

commission: a book of indulgences, the dreams
of a wide-eyed monk, on the up in Wittenberg.

# Harbouring

*'. . . flotsaming words, harbours of time'*
— KELLY GROVIER

We sip sugared rice-tea
with the astologers of Kan-
balu, who calm the sea,

or at will raise tempests.
Over the jetty's hammered
bronze, the sea's sus-

urrations speak of a turn
in the wind, not grasping what
it means not to give ground

the slip. A parade floats
from the city like the holler
of leaf-monkeys, and ships'

bells clatter across water,
mingling with Emperor Wu,
who argues the is of now.

Beyond the quay's candles,
shapes move through waves,
finite, rapid, still far-flung.

# Umbels

*after Heinrich Heine*

## 1. HUSH-HUSH

Should I rat out
my girl, or grass her
up with metaphors?

In the flowery hut
there's a secret—still warm
and blushing. Fan its rosy

ashes. The world
doesn't believe in flames,
stops short of poetry.

## 2. SIREN

Up there—madam
with her comb and golden
hair spits notes

at the river. The ferry-
man understands, but
misses the rocks. Gulp him

waves—reef split
his boat. She'll do for him
with her cheesy grin.

## 3. PANG

My heart's had it
with old times, when
the world seemed habit-

able by friends. Familiar
lines have shifted
and nothing sticks. God's

gone cold, the devil's
dead—umbels of mould
spreading like a lover.

# Islands

*for Damian Walford Davies*

Let's ride to the Pineapple Islands,
build a dome on the shore;
seed the demi-green fringe,
sow the gilded sands. We'll raise
barricadoes, post look-outs, keep
the palpable world at bay;
foray into trackless woods,
to return with tales of monkey.

Let's ride to the Pineapple Islands—
plant steel on the circumference, lay
syntax, light fires, push skirts
and folds of the perfumed forest.

Let's ride to the Pineapple Islands.
Perhaps there'll be pineapple people.

# Amulet

Well-thought-out on a sofa, her polished
fingers hold a relation of pine and crane
to the light. Her speckled shades

are insect wings. Through stick windows,
cicadas whir and click, break in the heat.
There, just beyond the gemmed gates,

a layabout claps his gong for alms.
Of course, my girl's the lady of rank,
and I'm the deadbeat. The long-beaked

bird stares with the chilliness of art, its single
eye turned on man-like figures and mysterious
beasts, a mountain goat tethered to a tree.

# Thitherwards

What does the tramp
mouth? I sleuth
what it might mean

to drink coffee in the bones
of the city. A woman is
watching—now and again

I catch it, the song of her
eye. I'd like to show her
just what I'm up to. Far

from the forest's fluid cor-
culum, this place sews subtler
seeds I don't get the gist of.

# Old Man of Tang

What are you mulling
over on the heroned lake,
perched against the water's

bronze? Yin, if you
are he, I think your thoughts
wander from the temple carp

to the gates and fragrant pear
groves of the city, to the silken
women, whose gifts are golden

peaches, fat as goose eggs.
In the square, holy men huddle
round a three-legged *ding*,

and vendors peddle bean buns.
All afternoon, the air has clanged
with long-handled *nao* bells,

haunched, mouths-up in wooden
frames. Round-faced exorcists
demand strings of copper coins;

an illusionist turns herself first
to a bamboo stalk then into
a skull. No one sees the soused

librettist who daubs chit-chat
with a lip-thinned brush tipped
with rabbit fur. Wise to his pipe-

dreams, the jaded throng shrugs
his crotched accents, preferring
timeless tales of rain.

# Beach

That's not surfing,
says the girl in the pink
cap. He's in the shallows,

sliding on shingles,
skiffing with his poly-
styrene board, not yet out

of depth in the whorls,
but tiny against the salt
cracking on pebbles.

    ~

We find a wrecked crab
among the curios,
antique in the tide,

prise the tiny hinge
of its hammer claw. I
sketch the ground

and moon, explain
the backlash, losing
my line at the equator.

# Garden

Tonight the garden's quiet,
its greenfringe skies
recently busy with patrols

of pilotless creatures—
curious, many-eyed drones
hoovering among the imp-

roved flowers, the repand rose,
and its strong peduncles—
the garden's thoughts

like cultivated seeds
laid out in tinder-
boxes round the borders.

# The Couple

*Sculpture by John de Andrea, 1978;*
*Ludwig Forum für Internationale Kunst, Aachen*

Up against a different wall, her skin
lurid, monochrome, hair
illusioning life; its absence his sole
theme. Stripped, contraposto,

what does she see in
him, the perfect dissembler?
Those lapels date him, his wide
slacks. Unmoved, he stares

into gallery space, blind
not to what she is, but
was. Her feet shadowing
wax, only the pressure

of flesh on clothes, the untanned
halo of last summer's
bikini, keep her here at all, re-
fusing art; still, impossibly.

# Brothel Scene
*Roman fragments, Glyptothek Munich*

Just a pair of knees, the tail-
end of a skirt, barely any elbow

room, settling into his chiselled
waist. The stone that says *stay*

*till this is over.* It's been done
with less attachment before;

and perhaps those capable
thighs don't altogether object

to having the upper hand, the cent-
urian for all time making a fist of it.

## View at Le Gras
*First photograph, 1826*

Cap off, the little window opens
onto windows blackened by light,
to a pear tree with an inked sky.

That first exposure makes a tarn-
ished mirror of the yard. The patio's
empty. Just the cool geometry of stone.

Yet plainly someone's in, thinking
of pewter washed in lavender oil,
rays hardening on the plate. Together,

now, a dovecote, the long low roof
and chimney of the bakehouse, two grainy
suns each side of the seven-hour frame.

# A Guide to the Stars

Fifteen and sixteen,
our brailed bodies
taut with clarity beneath

an alphabet of extinct
suns. Crowned with secrets,
we kissed in deferred lust-

er, figmented, present.
Later, we propped
ourselves on cryst-

alled grass, crossed
on a promise to the pebbled
house at the lane's end.

In all of this, the moon
is as it is, or was
a second ago—and neither.

# Steerage

So I hung them, the weathered
charts — two undecipherable
codes of sticks and shells —

as mute curios in the captain's
cuddy. Only a half-cut sailor,
egged-on by the rummed

loan of an officer's coat let
slip their secrets: *rilíbis* and *kae-*
*libs*, he slurred, species of waves

for which no word's been
coined in landlocked tongues.
These, he drifted, pointing

to the mussels, are islands,
and these, something darker.
Now, no navigator dares

consult such groundless
superstitions, only a wizened
blue-jacket, three sheets

to the wind, still turns to them
from time to time to keep
his compass spinning.

RMT. KG.

# Delft Tile

Fired on white tin glaze,
tessellated to abstraction, it's
the same quiet always.

Drainage mills stuck half-
tilt on the polders, water gaining
weight in the tail-race, three pounced
skiffs missing their pilots
in the low-lying afternoon.

Only stick pikemen, deft
like Chinese symbols, spell
inundation.

# Toads

Toad one sits four
square, smirks
at the mower, blades

a matter of sheer
indifference. The garden's
blowsy in the wind,

arms of blackberry arc-
ing over high walls
of cinereous rock.

Toad two sprawls
on spoils freshly blud-
geoned from the bank,

unflappable, sun
thickening behind beech,
apples blushing

with the plums.
Toad three stains
the kitchen, paratoid,

warty. We bale him
out in a shoebox.
Unmewed by the woodpile,

he floplollops
into mulch, blessings
on his lumpy head.

# Porcelain Dish

On the spandreled bridge,
ringed with dragons
and willow branches,
a boy and his brocaded

girl count ship-lapped
junks back from the ducts
and sieves, watch sailors
weigh their one-

fluked wooden anchors
in the bay. In the still
suspended moment, a jade
disc falls into the vitrified

stream, an equilibrium of water-
dragging light. Around the trans-
fixed pair, glazed masks,
crouching beasts fired by fire.

# Dissolution

Who believed the official line? Hell.
It always came down to the gravity
of lead. He ordered the liquidization

of capital; plate and heavy stone vanished
like coiling incense from a censer.
We suffered Layton's swagger, Leigh's puffed

roiling—*bad women in the precincts, super-*
*stitious relics swapped for cash.* Blind
to the curve of our tympanum, the endless

arcade of the chapter house, the grace
of our fan-vaulting, they nobbled
the new boys with questionnaires,

leaving with the Holy Cross, a gold phial
of the Virgin's milk, three coals
that braised St Lawrence sweet and black.

# Vaulting

As difficult as it looks,
if you look closely;
to fix weight's floating

point. You ask why
it won't collapse
inwards to its centre,

and I say haunches,
groin over bay. Truth is,
it wants to fall. But

make the stones wide
at the top, the curve just
so, it can't: each arris

a perfect metaphor,
the intersecting X-
shapes heavenly figures.

When it works,
you almost don't
need walls. Just windows,

and light—stained
for the effect of true
presence; a combination,

with or without ribs,
that may be relied on
in unbattened days.

# Where *c* is the speed of

1.

Let light be emitted
from the light-emitting
device, and we arrive

at the problem of distance
(we talked about it earlier).
Consider a ray. Let it be

placed at right angles
to an observer, a single part-
icle careening through

dark. Now you unpick it,
vectors—tensors—
yielding the vanished

clock, the clock at rest,
the moving clock,
whose time is unknown.

Do this in memory of.

2.

We continue our analysis
of actions committed
outside the light.

That part we call the future,
and the past, or the accu-
mulation of time, is also

omitted for brevity—
our concern the precise
present. Beyond doubt

the equation that proves
things are in a state
of acceleration. We feel

its physical meaning without
exact solutions; it's enough
just to write it down.

Is it not true that the age
of tomorrow's universe
will be the same as it was

yesterday, or is today?
There is in all things
a truth that is true,

and a lie that's true, also